Words

A simple reflection

Amy Churchouse

**First published in 2020 by
Doing Things Differently**

The words in this book will take you on an adventure. An adventure which may take you in many different directions, all of which you are encouraged to explore, if you so wish. It may bring realisations and new perspectives. Some of the questions may have answers for you that are interesting and others that are challenging.

This journey is yours and will deliver what you allow it to. Please take your time and proceed with curiosity. Reflect and explore with compassion and without judgment. Discover what might be possible with new awareness and a deeper understanding. These words have been written to create opportunities. Where they take you will depend on how you engage with them.

And they all start with a simple reflection...

Words.

What do they do for us?
What do they do to us?

Where do they take us and
what do they bring us?

What would we have
and what would we do,
if they were taken away?

So many words.

What do they mean?
And to who and why?

Where did we pick them up, learn about what they mean and how
does that change the way we feel about them?

Or the people they are attached to.

What do they tell people about us?
And are they right?

So simple, a combination of letters.
Yet they carry so much expectation, power and responsibility.
So much potential for understanding.

And for misunderstanding...

Do they speak the truth?
Or do they only describe someone's perspective?

Do we believe them? And why is that?

Because we trust them?
Or because we trust who said them?

Because we understand?
And how do we know we understand...?

Before there were words
there were humans.

What would happen if we
took the words away?

Did you get that name at birth or at school?
Or did you decide you liked a different name altogether?

Did you change it when you got married?
Double barrelled or kept your fathers?
And why did you keep your fathers?

What does that say about you?

What can I know about you when you introduce yourself?

Mr, Mrs or Ms?

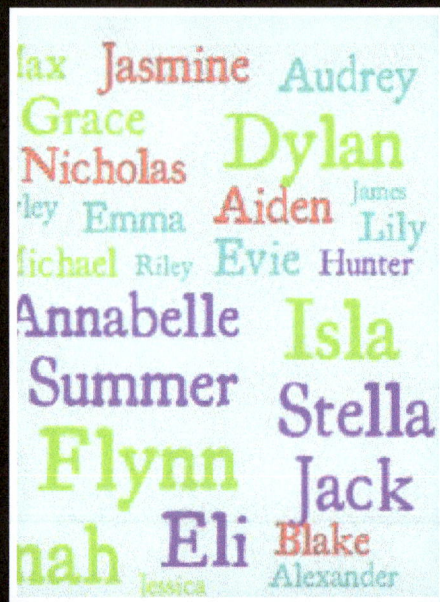

How would you describe yourself?

To yourself?

And to others?

What words would you use?
What do they mean to you?
And what do they mean to me?

Why did you choose those words?

Did someone tell you you were strong, weak, smart or a geek?
Did that become a part of the description?

Or a part of your human?

Did those words help you or hold you back?
Did you even notice?

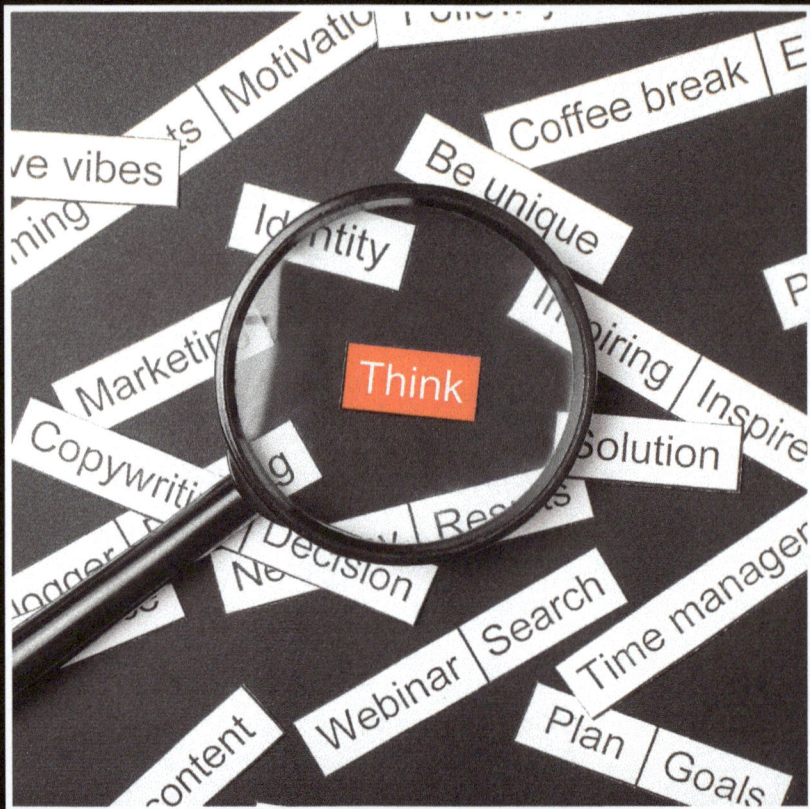

Before there were words
there were humans.

What would happen if we
took the words away?

Labels are words.

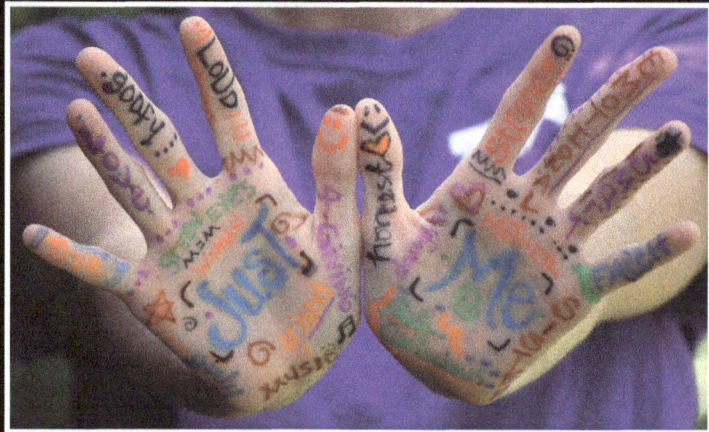

What are the labels you wear?

Were they given to you, attached by you,
or assumed by others based on how you are?
Or how you appear?

Do they do a good job telling everyone about you?

Or do they unintentionally package you with other things?
With other people?

And are those other people really like you?

Are these labels words you use because then other peop
Will they know you?

Or are these labels you choose because it helps them to
understand?

Because you are proud?

Because these words make you feel strong?
Because they protect you?
Because it makes things easier?

Easier for you or only for them?

Or passionate? Or stubborn? Or staunch? Committed?
Or maybe they got hurt?

Do these words help us to connect with them?
To learn? To understand?

Or does that depend on how these words are worn?
Or who is wearing them?

dis·ci·pline[1] /'dɪs
..., does not o
mind and charact
of obedience

Professional, corporate, tradie?
Unemployed, volunteer...?

Description? Label? Vocation?
Or just words?

Which one are you and what does that say about you?

What opportunities does it offer you?
Or maybe take away from you?

Does it say that you're smart? Or skilled?
Or stupid? Or lazy?
That you like working hard?

Or does it depend on who you are talking to?
And who they know?

And what they know?
About you...

Or what they know about being professional, corporate,
a tradie, unemployed or a volunteer.

Before there were words
there were humans.

What would happen if we
took the words away?

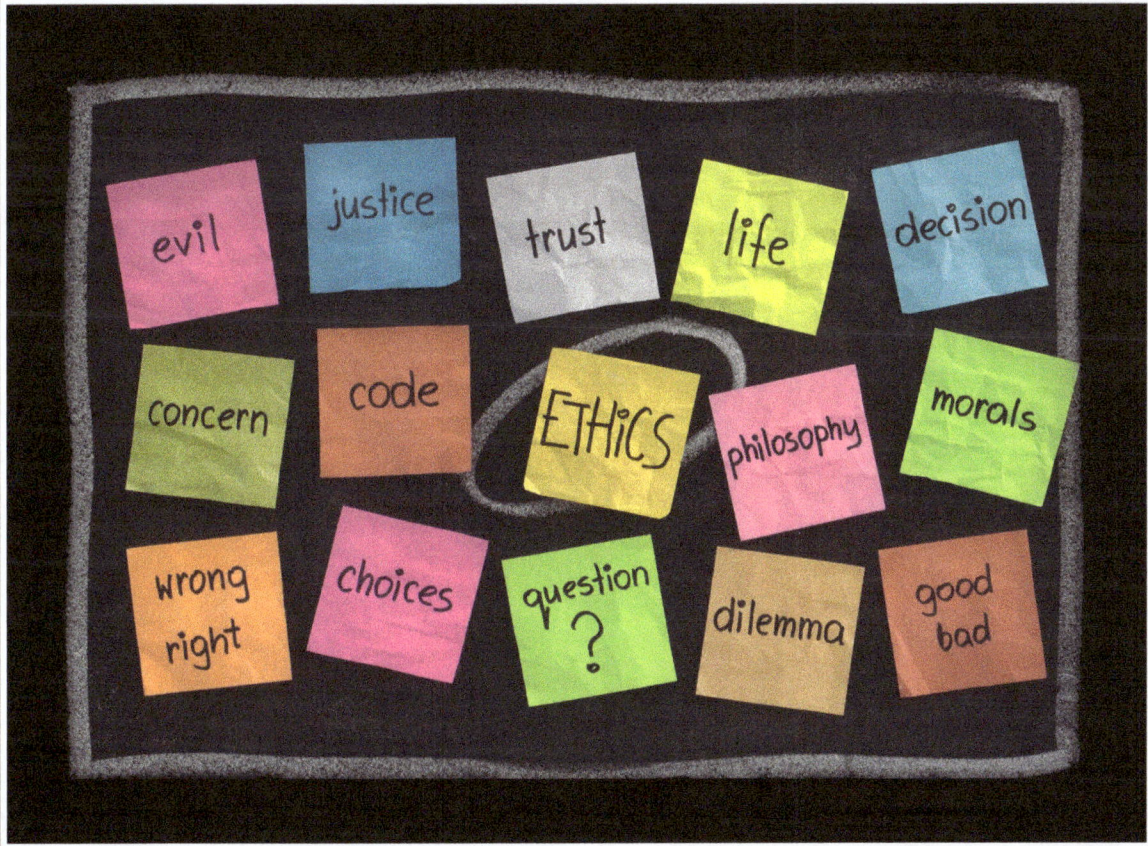

Feelings are words.

What is that you are feeling?

Do you describe it as anxiety?
Or excitement? Or energy?
Or is it adrenalin?

Angry. Sad. Happy. Scared?

How do you feel when you say that is how you are feeling?

Does using that word make you feel good or bad?
Better or worse?

What do you decide to do with that?
And how do you know what to do?

Did someone's words help you know?

"How are you?"

FINE

confused betrayed / useless / broken / never good enough / fragile anxious i'm falling apart and / you don't notice it / pathetic annoying / rejected / lonely / defeated

How do you feel when someone uses these words?

Anxiety, depression, trauma, survivor...

Maybe a doctor?
Or a friend?
Or your mother?

Do you believe them?
Do you believe what you feel? Or what you see?

How do you know what to believe?

Gender, sex, identity.

More words.

Woman, man, cis, trans, non-binary?
Intersex?

He, she, they?
Gay, straight, bi, queer, asexual, lesbian?

Do they tell your story? Or state your position?

Or is it just a description?
Does it matter?

Why is that?

How much of your story do these words share?

Did they get you kicked out of home?
Married three times?
Pregnant too young?

Did they make you like sport? Trucks or dolls?
Or want to have kids?

Do they describe how you like to connect?
To touch or to hold?

Or who you want to connect with?
Someone, everyone, anyone?
Or no one?

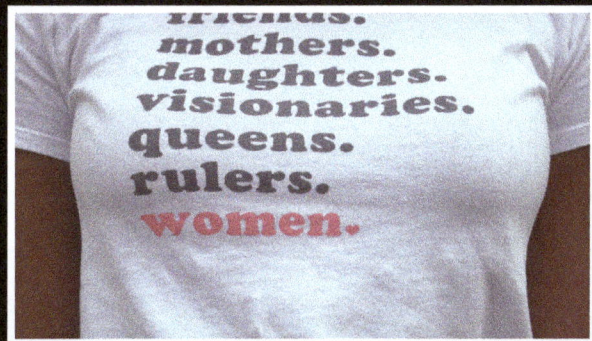

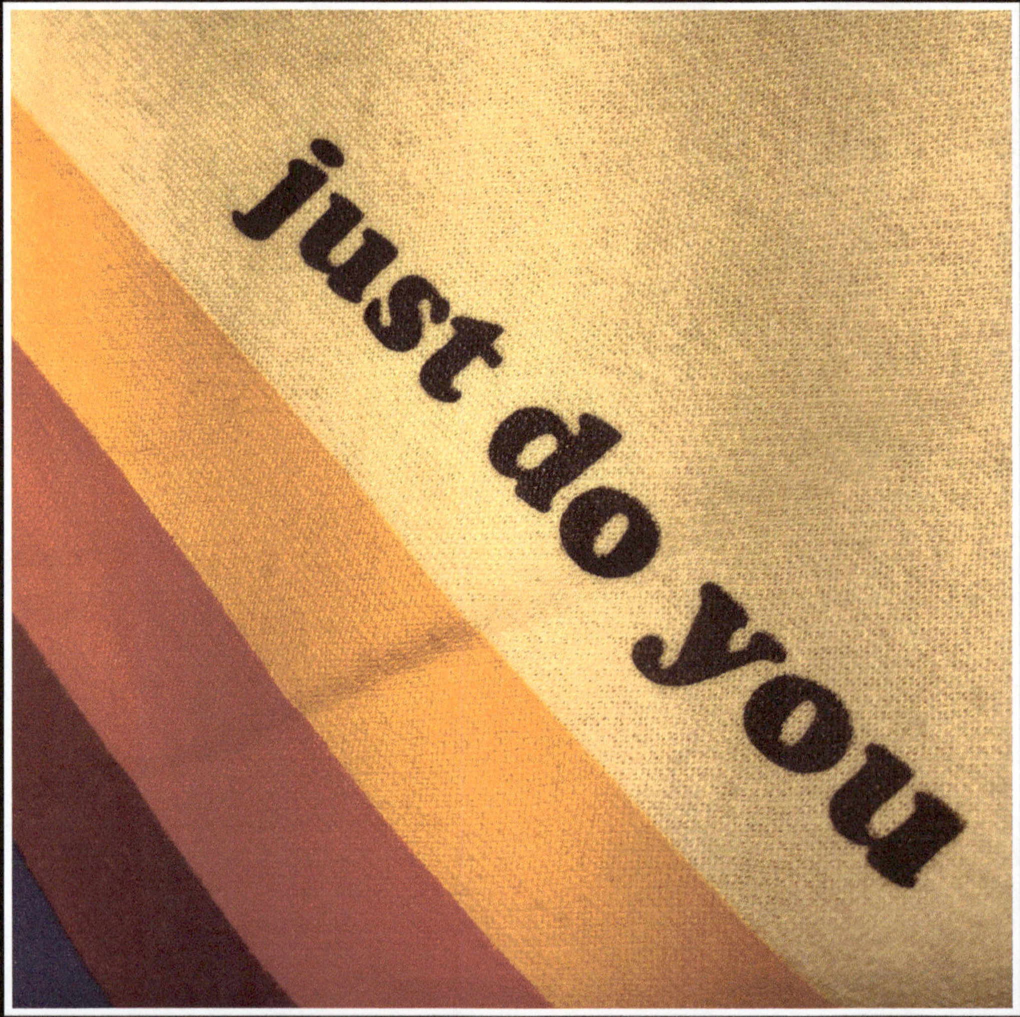
just do you

Monogamous.

Polyamorous.

How many and why?
Now or back then or forever?

How do you know and why is that so?

Do these words create boundaries for you?
Or barriers for others? Or both?
How does that work for you?

Have you thought about how it might be to wear the other word?
To explore the other word?

If you did, would you use the word?
And what new words would you need to know to do so?

Before there were words
there were humans.

What would happen if we
took the words away?

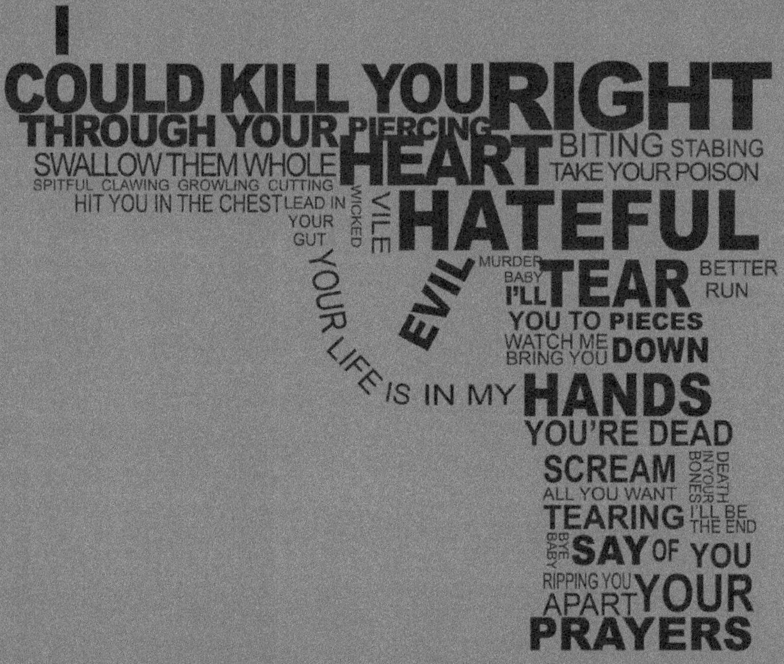
I
COULD KILL YOU RIGHT
THROUGH YOUR PIERCING HEART
BITING STABING
TAKE YOUR POISON
SWALLOW THEM WHOLE
SPITFUL CLAWING GROWLING CUTTING
HIT YOU IN THE CHEST LEAD IN YOUR GUT
WICKED
VILE
HATEFUL
EVIL
MURDER
BABY
I'LL TEAR
YOU TO PIECES
BETTER RUN
WATCH ME BRING YOU DOWN
YOUR LIFE IS IN MY HANDS
YOU'RE DEAD
SCREAM
DEATH IN YOUR BONES
ALL YOU WANT
TEARING
I'LL BE THE END
BYE BABY
SAY OF YOU
RIPPING YOU APART
YOUR PRAYERS

Safe.

What does that mean?
And who to?

Will you be safe?
Is that place safe?
And what makes it so?
According to who?

Perhaps you mean what are the risks?

And then don't the risks depend on the person?

How much they know?
And how big they are?
Who they are connected with and what skills they have?

If we are 'safe', or they are 'safe' or somewhere is 'safe', what does that mean we can do?

How do we engage?

With confidence?

With no fear?

Do we question?

Are we open?

Curious?

Paying attention?

Staying aware?

Are we really safe?

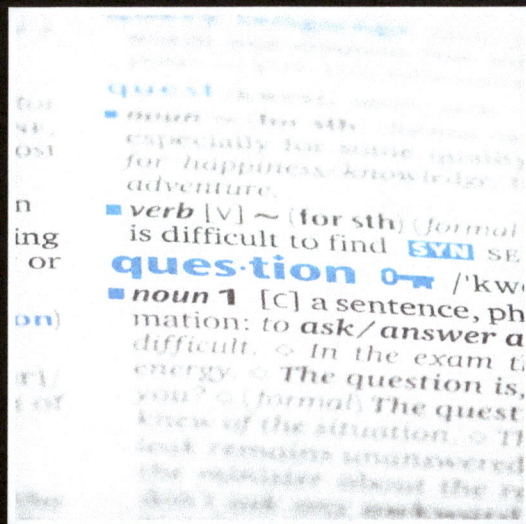

Why do you work?
Why do you do that work?

Do you enjoy it?
Tolerate it? Or resent it?

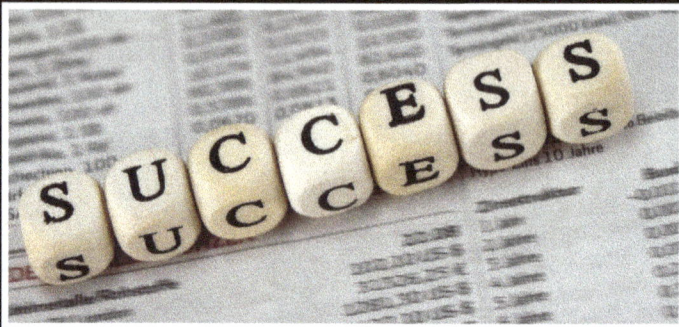

Is it learning?

Growing? Creating? Exploring? Questioning?
Progress? Contribution? Determination? Pain? Improvement?
Connection? Belonging?

Security?

Are you sure?

Do you work for the pay?
The puzzle?
The power?
Or the prestige?

Or because it's important?

Because other people need you to?
Or because you think you need to?

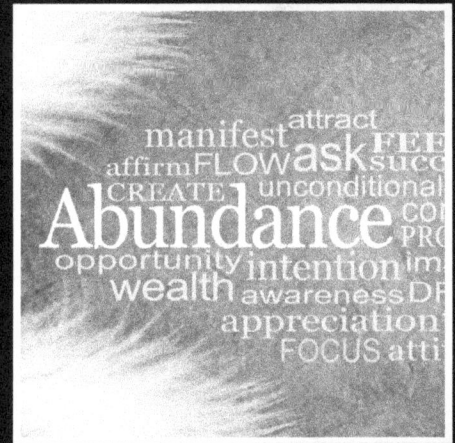

Before there were words
there were humans.

What would happen if we
took the words away?

UNDENIABLE
sweetheart lips
craving NEVERENDING relationship
extravagant WEDDING &
RAPTURE lust seek TRUST new ENJOY SPARK
enchant
emotion CARE fond feeling red
devote & affection PURE hot
ETERNAL CRUSH magic moments FOREVER !
AMOUR LOST SUGAR passion commitment bride
SADNESS FOREVER GOOD
longing purple ONE kiss favour playful
fond unrestrained infatuation
intense strong ave
care Your big ROMANCE
ecstatic TRUST PROPOSE promise sensual
LOVE
POTENTIAL MARRY I'm sorry RENDEZVOUS GESTURE hold
gain FANTASY vulnerable mate
BABY fire caress spouse ALLWAYS goodbye
beau NEVER MEMORY
BOY honey kid COUPLE CHERISH
favoured warm hands soulmate
perfect gift EMOTIONS MOTIVES SAFETY
life receive divine inclination
HEARTBEAT
you
SUNSHINE first
groom AFFAIR
JOY DATING involvement
provacative NOW FUTURE
PURPOSE
CONNECTION
beauty exotic FOND
OPEN SEX SUGAR GRACE
BLISS
TRUST DENIAL
arousing attachment loveable
REVEALING TOUCH TRUTH
HONEYMOON PAIN TOUCH
FEEL seductive
SOFT teardrop
EMBER delicate
companion FLAME
DARLING SOFT
girlfriend

Love.

Can you see it when you look at them?
When they do what they do?

Do you feel it?
When you do what you do?

Or is it just a word that you use?

I love you.

What does that mean?
When you say it?
When you hear it?

Or are they just some words that we say...?

Before there were words
there were humans.

What would happen if we
took the words away?

The ones we choose and those we hear?
And what will happen as a result?

Will they bring us together or disconnect us?

Will they keep us safe?
Help us belong?

Or alienate us?

Will they soothe or scar?
And how long for?

They are all just words.

Words I understand, and you understand.

Sometimes.

But often we don't, and then we don't know.
And then we don't know what to do.
Don't know how to feel, how to be...

Or what to say.

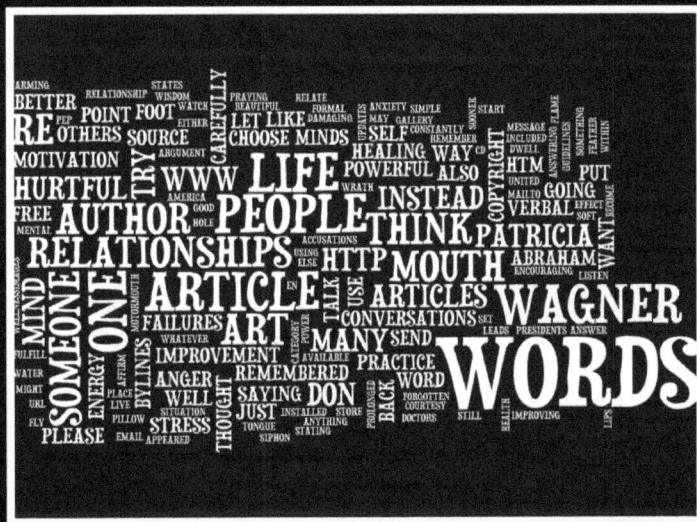

Before there were words
there were humans.

What would happen if we
took the words away?

Words Have Power

Epilogue

Where did these words take you?

Did they make you think about the words you use?
Or those that others choose?
About their depth and diversity of meaning?

About how they make you feel?
About how yours might be heard by other people?

About how damaging a misunderstanding can be?
And how unnecessary these are when they begin at the words?

About what words can achieve? Or destroy?

Did it make you want to learn more words?
Or to know what is behind the words?
Will you now explore further, listen closer or look deeper...?

What would you do if there were no words?
How would you connect?
How would you share?
How would you learn and how would you know?

The Sun Catherine Quarrel in the Sky

by
Astrid Listner

Illustrated by
Susanne Auschill

Astrid Listner
The Sun Catherine - Quarrel in the Sky,
Sunny reading adventures, vol. 1,
Illustrated by Susanne Auschill

Creative-Story
Safferlingstr. 5 / 134
D-80634 Munich
Germany
Tel.: +49 (0)89 / 12 11 14 66
Fax: +49 (0)89 / 12 11 14 68
info@creative-story.com
www.creative-story.com

Cover-design, layout and typesetting:
Creative-Web-Projects, Munich

ISBN: 978-3-95964-005-3

Legal Notices

Acknowledgement by the Author

My special thanks go to my editor, publisher and good friend. Thank you for your creative power, tenacity and genuine friendship.

For Mom & Dad

The Sun Catherine

A new day begins. Sun Catherine awakens. She cranes her neck, stretches and curiously looks over the hills.

Full of anticipation for the coming day, she is adjusting her sunbeams. She directs her rays over the fields, grassland and forests.

It is going to be a lovely day. Catherine wants to make sure of it. After all, the world needs her light and warmth. Because then, birds sing in the air, rabbits hop around and bees buzz their melody.

Suddenly! What was that on earth? Big shadows move over the fields.

Oh no! Cloud Felix approaches and cloaks Catherine. His cloud beard tickles Catherine in her nose. She sneezes.

"Hey, what is that supposed to mean?" Catherine blusters. "Why are you always doing that? Every time you take away my light and hinder my rays from spreading. Nature needs my light and my warmth. They are important for the earth, so that plants can grow and animals can find food."

"Oh, let me be in peace," grumbles Felix. This day, he is in an especially bad mood. "You are not so very important. Nobody needs heat. You make the air much too warm. While I make it rain and give cooling. I give the earth water. Without water there is no life on earth."

"My warmth lets the plants grow and my light motivates everyone and lets them start the day with a smile on their face."

But Felix ignores Catherine's objections and moves in front of her.

"Go away," the sun wails in vain.

15

William the wind comes and joins Felix and Catherine.

"Are you haggling again? Does a day go by when you are not at loggerheads with each other?"

"He started it." "She began." Both Catherine and Felix respond at the same time.

"Always the same with you two," Jacob sighs. "You know, you are both equally important. You are our daily companion, Catherine. Your warmth and your light are essential, because without you no day would be imaginable. The daily routine of all would get disturbed, if you were not there for us. It would be very, very cold on earth. Your energy provides us with warmth, light and brings life."

Catherine smiles all over. She is pleased with the words of William.

17

Felix meanwhile pouts and rolls his eyes in annoyance. His mouth is pressed together and he narrows his eyes.

"But you are also important for nature, Felix," William turns to the cloud now. "Your shadow cools the earth. When you let it rain, you provide water for all plants and creatures. Water is essential for all life on earth. You bring change to the sky and color it with fleecy clouds, cumulus and all forms of mist and fog. You also announce your big brothers, who bring changes in the weather like snow and hail."

Felix feels flattered and no longer is in such a bad mood.

19

"You are both important for nature, for the flora and fauna," William continues. "You are both part of the cycle of nature."

"Now you see," Catherine says triumphantly. "I am important."

"But not as important as I am," grumbles Felix.

And again the two of them start fighting.

The wind moans. "We won't make any progress this way," he thinks. But how could he convince the two that both of them were essential for nature?

"I have an idea," William cries out. Catherine and Felix curiously look at him.

"What kind of idea?" Catherine asks.

"Each one of you may rule the sky alone for three whole days. You rule for three days, Catherine, and you for three days, Felix. And afterwards, we all meet up here again."

Catherine and Felix are happy about this suggestion. They cheerily agree with it. Each of them wants to prove in their own three days, how important for nature they are.

The next day, Catherine awakens full of anticipation. She is happy that today for a change Felix will not vex her.

Eagerly she rises extra high up in the sky. She smiles from ear to ear and directs her rays down onto earth with special care. Today, she wants to prove herself.

Slowly, the earth awakens. The plants stretch up towards her; the animals come out of their dens.

Everyone smiles and is cheerful.

"Now you see, Felix," Catherine thinks. "Who wants rain, if one could have it so nice with me?"

Content, Catherine goes to sleep behind the hills in the evening. She is tired and happy.

The second day, Catherine tries even harder. But something seems different to the day before. The animals no longer are as carefree and the flowers let their heads droop a bit. A little rabbit looks at the sky with irritation and blows up his cheeks. He is sweating.

Catherine is wondering, why is the mood no longer as cheerful as yesterday, also the water in the river is less. But no, she won't let that stifle her mood and happily continues to shine.

On the third day, Catherine's mood is no longer so great. The river is parched and the animals are sweating and no longer leave their dens. Even the plants let their heads droop.

Catherine is brooding: "It is no longer so funny, when I am in the sky alone and my light and warmth reach nature unhindered."

She also must admit that it feels a bit lonesome up there in the sky all alone. Nobody is there, nobody to chat with.

A bit sad she sinks down behind the hills in the evening.

29

Today is the time for Felix. He can finally prove himself and show what he can do. Felix grumbles and lifts from behind the hills. The next three days he may slide in front of Catherine.

Puh, to dominate the sky all alone, that sounds exhausting and like lots of work. But Felix after all wants to prove that he is more important than Catherine. So he begins, puffs himself out in the sky in front of Catherine and lets it begin to rain.

Slowly, the water in the river rises again. The plants stretch their leaves in the direction of the rain drops and hungrily quench their thirst. The animals also enjoy the fresh air which the rain brings them from the sky.

"Hah," Felix thinks. "Now everyone can see what happens, when I am not there for three days. Already, everything is parched and nature aches under the heat. Because of me water comes to nature and brings relief. Oh, how good that is. I am so much more important than Catherine."

Content with himself, Felix ends his first day of sole work in the sky.

The second day, Felix again starts with zest. After all, the first day went wonderfully. So overnight he decided to make it rain a little more today.

But the flowers and bushes cover themselves from the raindrops falling down from the sky. The river has filled up nicely and is full again. Does the water reach the den of family Rabbit? Everything on earth is quite wet and Felix even thinks he sees some animals shaking water from their coats.

But Felix pushes his qualms aside. "It does not matter. This little bit of water has never had a bad effect before."

On his third day, Felix again lets it rain heavily. The river now definitely burst its banks. Fields and meadows are under water. No animals far and wide. All remain in their dens. Family Rabbit stands deep in water and tries to save their home from the deluge. The chilliness troubles the creatures. Bees, butterflies, birds and ladybugs, Felix has not seen them for a while.

His mood is bad. Even though he wanted so much to prove to Catherine that he was more important than her, he still did not mean to harm anybody.

On the seventh day, Catherine, Felix and William meet again.

"And now, you two?! How did it go, to be all alone in the sky?" William asks.

"In the beginning, it was wonderful," Catherine says. "The animals were cheerful and the plants enjoyed the warmth. But already on the second day, the animals moaned and the plants tried to turn away their leaves from the heat. The river began to lose its water.

On the third day, the animals suffered under the heat. It created chaos in their daily routine. The flowers sadly dropped their heads and the river was completely parched."

After a pause, Catherine added thoughtfully and in low voice: "It somehow was lonesome, so all alone in the sky."

William nods with understanding. "And how were your experiences, Felix?"

"It was a lot of work," Felix grumbles. "It was exhausting. I let it rain the first day. This brought relief to nature. The animals enjoyed the cooling down and the plants quenched their thirst. The river began to fill again with a bit of water.

The second day, the earth became less lively. The water started to bother the plants and the river was full.

On the third day, it was so wet that most animals were no longer able to leave their dens. Family Rabbit even in their own home stood feet deep in water. And the river burst its banks and everyone's life was thrown into chaos."

"Now you both *see*," William said with a smile. "Even when you two are so very different, nature needs you both. Only together can you two keep the balance and harmony. Only combined can you two give flora and fauna what they need for their daily life. You in accord can bring the plants to grow and prosper."

Catherine and Felix look at each other thoughtfully.

William continues: "Your difference is essential for nature. Each one of you may remain the way you are, no question about that. You need to understand that neither one of you is more important than the other. You need to work out a common way to be together. Take care to find a way to determine who may rule the sky when, because each one of you has an important task in the sky. Each of you has strengths and weaknesses and that is all right that way, but you must learn that only together can you make good things happen. Only together can you keep the world in balance and keep the cycle of nature intact."

The End

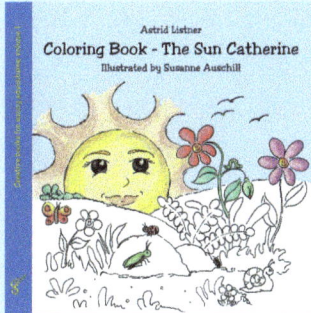

Creative supplement for all ages:

Coloring Book - The Sun Catherine
ISBN 978-3-95964-006-0

The adventures of

Catherine, Felix and William

continue in volume 2:

The Cloud Felix - Why Friends are Important
(Sunny reading adventures, vol. 2)
ISBN 978-3-95964-045-9

Coloring Book - The Cloud Felix
ISBN 978-3-95964-046-6

www.ingramcontent.com/pod-product-compliance
Lightning Source LLC
Chambersburg PA
CBHW041559260326
41914CB00011B/1322